5-MINUTE ART JOURNAL

5-MINUTE
ART
journal

QUICK PROMPTS
FOR CREATIVE INSPIRATION

Text and Illustrations by Collaborate Agency

R

ROCKRIDGE
PRESS

First Rockridge Press trade paperback edition 2022

Rockridge Press and the Rockridge Press logo are trademarks or registered trademarks of Callisto Media Inc. and/or its affiliates in the United States and other countries and may not be used without written permission.

For general information on our other products and services, please contact our Customer Care Department within the United States at (866) 744-2665, or outside the United States at (510) 253-0500.

Paperback ISBN: 978-1-68539-259-8

Manufactured in the United States of America

Designer: Linda Snorina
Cover and Interior Designer: Lisa Schreiber
Art Producer: Samantha Ulban
Editors: Lauren Bonney and Kelly Koester
Production Editor: Caroline Flanagan
Production Manager: David Zapanta

10 9 8 7 6 5 4 3 2 1 0

This journal belongs to

....

Introduction

Welcome to this *5-Minute Art Journal*! Within these pages, you'll find 300 art prompts to draw, sketch, create, and consider. Each prompt encourages you to tap into your own expression, creativity, and style, and you don't have to follow the prompts exactly. Have fun with them; choose a prompt and complete it in a way that inspires you. That's bound to be different from the way it would inspire someone else—and that's the beauty of art. It's not about getting it perfect; rather, it's about taking time every day to create something. Watching your artistic skills grow over the year should be considered a by-product, not the aim, of this book.

UNLEASHING YOUR CREATIVITY IN 5 MINUTES

In this journal, you'll find starting points to get you creating. While most of the prompts will involve drawing, coloring, painting, or doodling, some are writing prompts. They'll all help you think in new and creative ways.

Whether you're a regular at artistic activities or a first-time creator, there's so much to gain from setting your creative side free. Not only will you improve your artistic abilities, but by sitting down and doing a single, enjoyable task for just five minutes a day, you will also be practicing mindfulness—something that's been scientifically proven to improve your mental and physical health, as well as your concentration.

We're all so entrenched in our daily routines. Engaging in the same brain patterns every day will produce the same results. But looking at tasks in a new way can help you with problem-solving in other parts of your life, too. It's possible to feel calmer and happier by being creative; emotions can be released, leading to greater self-awareness.

5 TIPS FOR 5-MINUTE ART

1. **Make time:** Making time can be tough—we all have busy lives. But there are many little pockets of in-between time where you might find a spare five minutes: a moment between chores, during a lunch break, on a commute, waiting for a kettle to boil, or as you're getting ready for bed. First thing in the morning is a great time to be creative, too.

2. **Make space:** Find a spot in your home you can go to and get creative: a corner of your kitchen table or desk, a space on the floor of your bedroom, or, if it's nice weather outside, perhaps a garden chair or the porch, or a bench in a nearby park. Make this your official creative space, and when you go there, you'll put yourself in the right frame of mind.

3. **Don't overthink:** These exercises aren't about producing beautiful works of art or fabulous poetry (though if you get something pretty out of it, that's great). Don't stress and don't spend ages thinking about how you're going to complete the day's mini project. Read the prompt and just get started. Let your imagination take you wherever it decides to go.

4. **Flip around:** You can work through this book in whatever way you like. You absolutely do not have to start on the first prompt and complete the book from beginning to end. Some days you might be in the mood to do a little writing, other days drawing, some days a larger page, others a half page. It's all okay. Work on the task you're inspired by that day. If you're one of those people who likes to complete a book from beginning to end, that's fine, too.

5. **Try something new:** Don't be afraid to try something you wouldn't normally do. Never tried making a collage? Give it a go. Don't think of yourself as a writer? Why not see what happens? No one is going to judge you or grade this, so take these projects as an opportunity to try something . . . and even fail at it. That's how we learn, right?

MATERIALS AND SUPPLIES

You do not have to spend a ton of money on fancy art materials to get creative. You might want to gather pencils (color and/or graphite) and all sorts of pens. Working in ballpoint pen creates its own unique look. Whatever you have at home will work—thick markers, fountain pens, crayons, paint, charcoal, anything.

You could do some of these projects as collages, using images from printed sources or found objects. However you choose to get creative, set your mind free and see what happens.

THEMES FOR INSPIRATION

Creative inspiration can come from anywhere. There are the usual places you'd think of as inspirational, like museums and photography, poetry and novels, nature and the outdoors. But why not try looking for inspiration in places you wouldn't normally expect to find it: the supermarket, traffic, a child's finger painting, or a scientific journal, for instance? When you actively seek out inspiration, you'll be amazed where you'll find it.

Don't worry if you're struggling to feel inspired—this journal is here to help.

HOW TO USE THIS BOOK

In this book, you'll find 300 prompts that will stimulate you to create something new. Each should take only five minutes—a short break from the busyness of life to focus on something else and get creative. You could set a timer for five minutes, but don't be too rigid about it.

Inside you will find:

- 238 complete-the-picture prompts, where a picture has been started and you will complete it and/or color it in.

- 52 from-scratch prompts, where you will start with a blank page and create an image using ideas from the prompt.

- 10 writing prompts, where you will be asked to write something creative.

Depending on what you're creating and what materials you're using to create it, it might be better to complete some prompts on a separate piece of paper. For example, you might decide to use thick acrylic paint one day, which would work best on thicker paper. Similarly, collages might make the book a little hard to close. But if you're okay with that, it's all fine.

To reiterate, you can complete these tasks in whatever way you choose. If a writing prompt inspires you to draw, then draw. If a drawing prompt asks you to shade something and give it dimension, but you prefer to paint in flat color, go for it. This is *your* book, and each prompt is designed to be completed in whatever way you want. Just enjoy yourself and get creative in the way that works best for you.

Think about the journey a leaf takes after it's fallen from its branch. Try depicting some leaves being carried by a brisk autumn wind. Including different angles, positions, and leaf types (or colors) could add variety and life to the scene.

Pointillism involves creating an image using a series of dots, with minimal lines (the paintings of Georges Seurat are great examples). Use a limited color palette or different shades of gray to illustrate a turtle using the pointillist style.

Capture the essence of an earlier era by designing covers for these vinyl records. Make them look retro, possibly even a themed set by the same musical artist.

Practice capturing flames that are frozen in time by finishing this campfire art. Use flowing lines to suggest motion and energy.

Imagine watching TV late at night and the way the light casts a glow across a dark room. Add stark shadows to create a late-night vibe. You could even add an ominous shadow to the scene to give it a moment of drama.

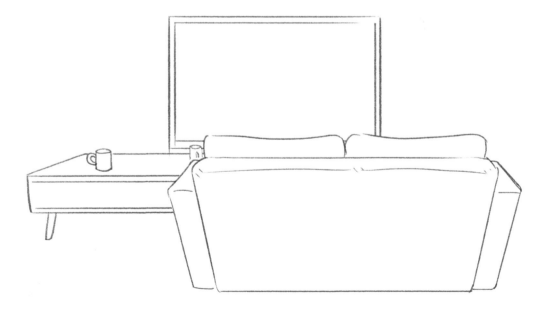

Fill in this cityscape skyline by drawing windows and other openings. You could even experiment by showing silhouettes in some of the windows and/or adding features to the rooftops and the sky.

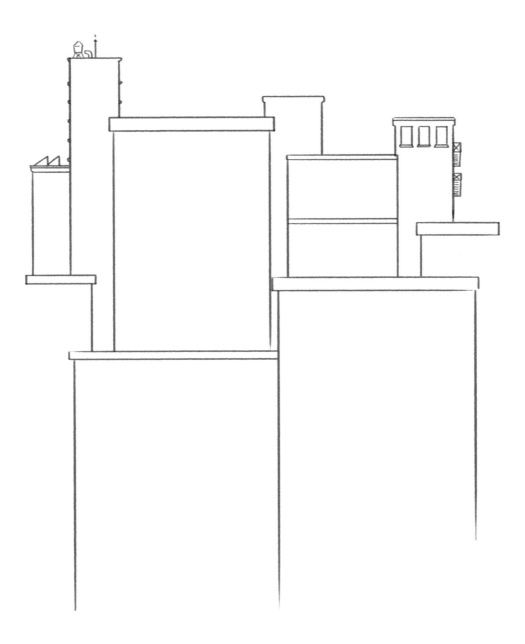

You probably handle coins every day, but have you ever observed the details that differentiate them? Draw a small assortment of coins, perhaps at different angles, and capture the subtle details you can only notice up close.

A haiku is a highly structured poem with just three lines. The first line has five syllables, the second has seven syllables, and the third has five syllables. Write a haiku about whatever you are feeling in this moment.

Use this space to illustrate the theme "cat scratch."

Fill in each stripe with a different pattern and/or gradient to give this a 1990s shopping mall vibe.

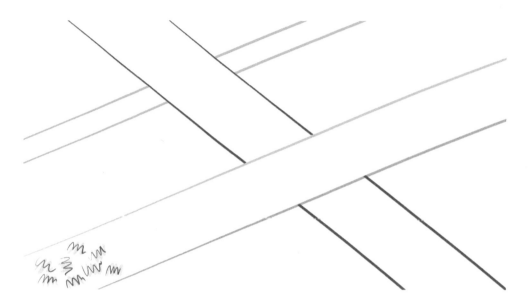

Hygge is a Danish concept that refers to the comfort, coziness, and quiet in simple things. Try illustrating the text and the space around it to express this concept so that someone who doesn't know the word's meaning might understand it.

Think of your favorite snack foods and drinks, and draw them together here. Don't dwell on details; focus on making them recognizable, and try to have fun with the composition.

Working in stylized type, design the title of an event in a way that illustrates its vibe.

You're Invited to

Add face paint, headwear, and/or props to these very engaged sports fans.
Make sure they match up thematically to show they're rooting for the
same team.

Add a paragraph to this story.

I had been waiting for them to return for days now, wondering how we'd get out of this mess. Just when I thought I might give up all hope, there was a knock.

Illustrate an ancient-looking treasure map. Base it on your own home or a local public space and see if you can follow it with someone.

Finish this trail of paw prints in the snow.

Illustrate this type with art that makes it appear lush and overgrown with vegetation.

OVERGROWN

Give this waterfall detail, but hide something special and secret behind the cascade.

Use a crosshatching technique (fine lines that intersect to create texture and shading—Rembrandt's sketches are a good reference) to fill this space with a still-life drawing of an object that is precious to you.

Design a trophy for an unconventional award you would win, if it existed.

Connect some dots in this night sky scene to portray a constellation of your own creation. You could focus on finding a unique object or creature, or perhaps go with a simpler constellation but add some style in how you present it.

Take it easy and enjoy using patterns and/or colors to fill in these circles. You could combine the effects you use where the circles intersect or incorporate all-new elements in those spaces.

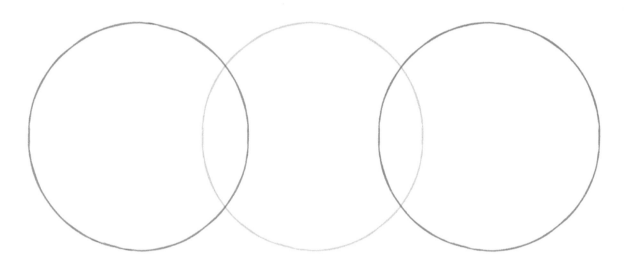

Try reading your own fortune. What do you predict could happen to you tomorrow, next week, or next year?

Pick your favorite breed of cat (domestic or otherwise) and illustrate the face of one in an impressionist style. This involves using many small strokes or lines laid out in ways that blend to imply shapes, shading, and form. (Claude Monet is a good reference for this style.)

Imagine floating in this canoe. Illustrate the surroundings; is it drifting on a slow and winding stream, heading down the rapids, or in the middle of a large lake?

Give rich shadows to the dark side of this moon, possibly using some form of blending and mixing to create an expressive, blurred effect.

Using shading and, if you'd like, color, make this still life scene feel warm. Perhaps go for a desert-like feeling.

Re-create a still frame from a scene in one of your favorite movies. Don't worry about making it totally accurate.

Illustrate a cross section of earth here, putting something surprising or unexpected just below the surface.

This empty page was torn from a magic potion book. Add illustrations for the ingredients that are mixed together to make this potion and give your mystical concoction a name.

Using your nondominant hand (or someone else's) as a reference, practice illustrating a human hand in any pose you please. Hands can be difficult, but they also don't need to look perfect to convey body language.

Design a pattern for these sneakers that suits your sense of fashion.

Complete this image to go along with the phrase "ready for an adventure."

Illustrate this type with art that makes it look like ruins that are cracked and crumbling.

Using whatever techniques you wish, add dimension and detail to this shrubbery. Hide someone or something inside, peeking out.

Create a piece of abstract art showing the idea of a wildlife sanctuary. You could create a scene, a logo, a pattern, or just abstract art of animals you'd expect to see in such a place.

Give this lion a magical mane based on the elements—electricity, fire, ice, water, wind, or stone. Choose one (or a few) and design the mane to fit this theme.

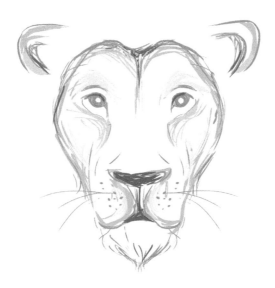

Complete this image to go along with the phrase "my bundle of joy."

Think of a high-stakes moment of action—a sporting event, a movie scene, or something you experienced firsthand—and try re-creating it at the moment of highest tension.

Imagine your ideal home. Is it a cozy cottage or something sleek and futuristic? Use this foundation as a starting point to build from.

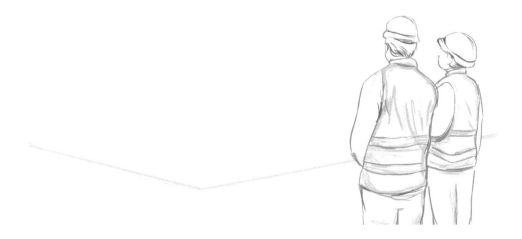

Use this grid to create a mosaic pattern. This activity works best with a range of colors, but varying shades of a single color can work, too.

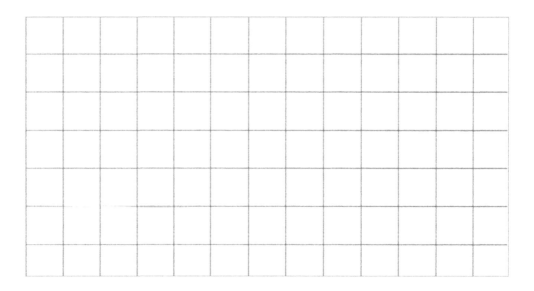

Using colors, lines, and/or any techniques you wish, fill in and perhaps surround or enhance this word with art that shows what feelings the word inspires in you.

Using the word "cloth" as your prompt, illustrate an object (or the word itself) draped in fabric. Consider how to depict the folds using classical Greek or Roman sculpture as a reference.

Give this mechanical robot toy a companion. You could design another model in the same style or create a robot of a different type altogether.

Add to this diner scene to make it feel like the earliest hours of the morning, before the sun is up.

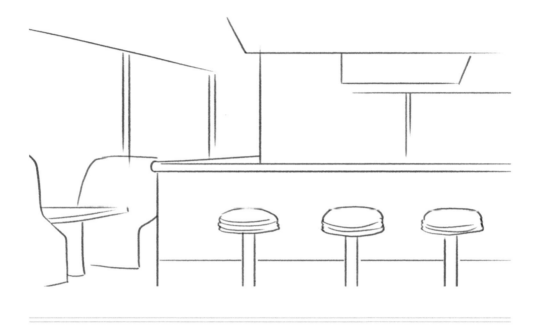

Using a single, continuous line, illustrate a person's face. Think before you start about the path you will take to keep the line from getting too messy. You could look up some examples of one-line art if you're not sure how to go about it.

Using the prompt "having a ball," create a sports scene centered around this ball. Think of how to portray a sense of movement and action rather than photorealism.

Using shading and, if you like, color, make this still life scene feel cool. Perhaps try for a snow-swept setting.

Write a paragraph about your first memory of going to the movies. Who did you go with? What did the cinema smell like? What were the seats like? Did you get any snacks?

This person is telling a scary ghost story late at night. Add lighting to their face to make the scene even more scary as their flashlight shine upward.

Take a nearby object to use as a reference and reimagine it as a furry creature or overgrown with grass or moss.

Illustrate the details of this stack of unopened mail. See if you can make each item look like it's from a different sender, and try to create a sense of lighting to suggest what time of day it is.

Add curtains to this window. Try to create a sense of transparency, with some light coming through, or focus on the shape of the fabric, with a sense of motion from wind blowing, or just try to design a set of curtains.

Using the word "fluff" as your prompt, draw what comes to mind—abstract, still life, whatever moves you.

Draw a comic strip depicting something interesting or exciting you experienced this week. Consider what will be in the dialogue boxes as you plan the story.

Package on the way! Fill in the branding on the side of this delivery truck with a real or made-up company you'd like to receive something from. What can you show about their products through the design on their truck?

Fill this tub with a fluffy bubble bath. Try to make the bubbles feel detailed and rich, foaming up out of the tub.

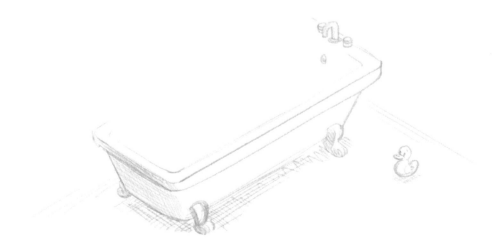

Create a piece of abstract art on the theme of a rocky mountain climb. Rely more on shapes, lines, and color rather than detail or shading. Think about how to frame your illustration in a unique way that captures your impressions of the experience.

Add shading and details to this deer. Consider how to create a sense of time of day using light and shadow, as well as distinguishing the texture of the fur and the antlers.

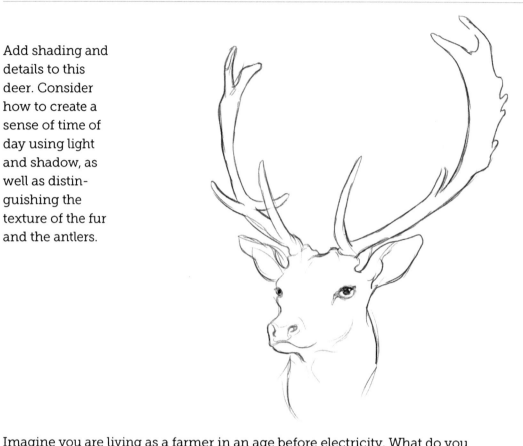

Imagine you are living as a farmer in an age before electricity. What do you farm? How does your typical morning begin? Describe some of the sensations you feel.

Add the details to these bundles of yarn and, if you'd like, color them to give them a rich depth.

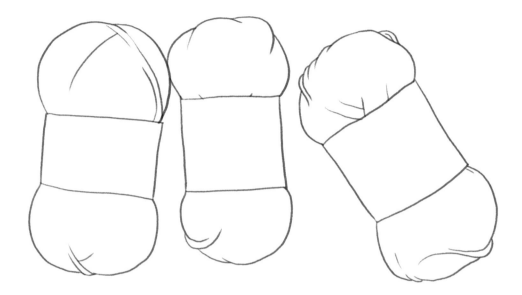

Fill this space with a cluster of meteorites. You could illustrate them drifting in space or burning up in an atmosphere. Do it by focusing on color, movement, detailed texture, light and dark, and shading.

Practicing a basic technique can be useful, and shading is a core skill. Add gradients of shade, as well as shadows, so these shapes all appear to have the same light source shining on them.

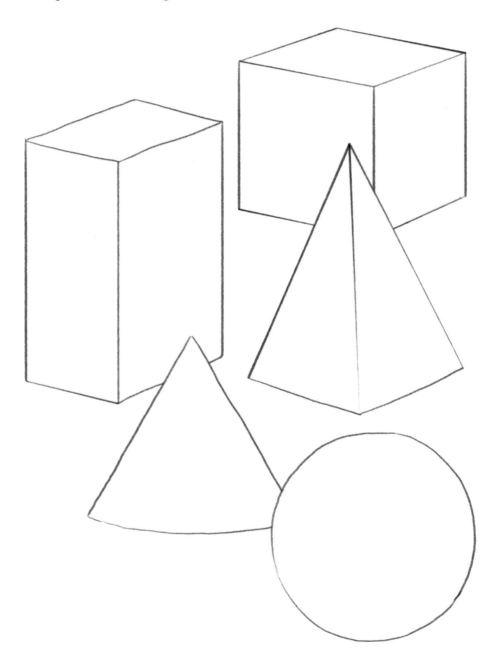

Using one or more of your own fingerprints, create an illustration of a creature. If you can't use your actual fingerprint, start with an outline of your finger(s).

Take the meal shown here and draw an almost finished version of it—as if someone had their fill and couldn't quite finish it.

Depict a desert scene with sand dunes or pyramids. You could try something abstract and simple, relying on contrast or color, or a more naturalistic style.

Give this cat furry detail and shading. Consider what time of day it is and what kind of lighting is in the scene.

Add a neon sign. You could focus on typography to create something unique-looking or concentrate more on using color to create a vibrant sense of lighting.

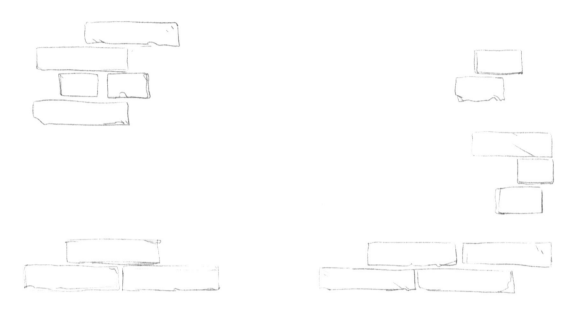

Help these two commemorate an occasion by giving them drinks to toast with, considering the moment the glasses clink as you add the liquids.

Give this very good dog some detail, including shading and fur texture. Give those wrinkles some character.

Using these spirals as a base, create some abstract art.

Imagine what simple kitchenware might look like in the far-off future, or even another dimension. Design and illustrate items such as utensils, cups, and bowls for this alien setting.

Fill these pieces of amber with some fossilized life-forms.

Design a futuristic and fancy motorcycle for this racer.

Design an unconventional sandwich or burger, showing the different ingredients suspended between the two halves of the bun, like a detailed breakdown of its construction.

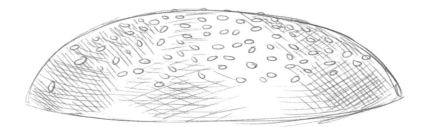

A metal spoon catches light in interesting ways. Try using one to study your own reflection from both sides and re-create what you see here.

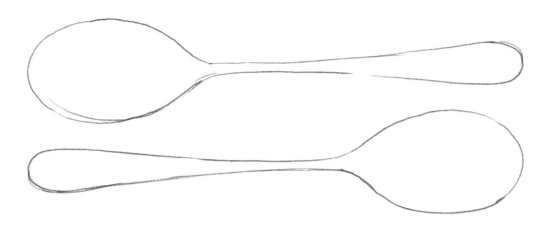

Add an eye-catching outfit to this runway model, basing the design on one or more objects nearby that you can use as a reference.

Add art to this pottery inspired by the style of ancient Greece. Perhaps depict a more modern-day legend or myth.

Write a funny two-line poem. Be as silly as possible—but it must rhyme.

Create a piece of abstract art on the theme of a hike in the woods. Rely more on shapes, lines, and color rather than detail or shading. Think about how to frame your illustration in a unique way that captures your impressions of the experience.

Scientists try to imagine what creatures looked like based on their fossilized remains. Looking at this creature's skeleton, how might you imagine it looked? Build the creature on top of its skeleton.

Fill this space with a wall of plants and flowers. It could be a repeating pattern, or each section could be totally unique.

Make this room look like a crazy party just swept through. What kind of party was it, and what sort of mess was left behind?

Try depicting each piece of candy after it's been unwrapped. You could also illustrate the wrappers after they've been removed.

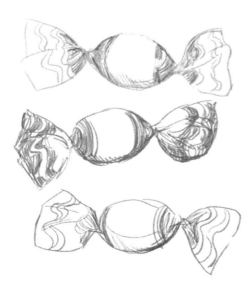

Try adding an effect of fog or mist to this lake scene. What techniques and what materials will you use to create the effect?

Imagine a common house-hold tool as if it was being cataloged by an alien archaeolo-gist. Is its purpose self-evident, or would they think it had a different purpose from the one it actually has?

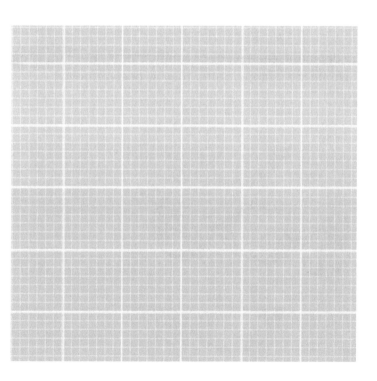

Give this mountain landscape detail. Think of ways to add a three-dimensional feeling to it for a more naturalistic appearance.

Using color, lines, and/or any techniques you wish, fill in and perhaps surround or enhance this word art to depict your own interpretation of what feelings the word inspires.

Illustrate some clay pottery that's been molded by hand. You can play around with a unique shape, focus on capturing texture and how light and shadow might play on it, or make something glazed and shiny.

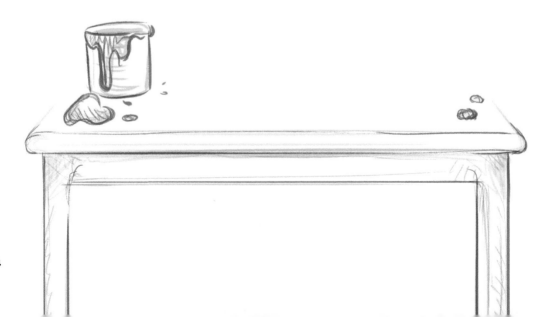

Take a sheet of paper, a napkin, a paper towel, or anything that's normally flat and not rigid, and crumple it up. Now use it as a reference and draw it. This can help give you some practice depicting folds and wrinkles.

Illustrate some animals that make sense for a savanna setting. If you're having difficulty deciding, some creatures that live on the savanna include zebras, cheetahs, elephants, and warthogs.

Add any type of athlete to this scene, but do so using abstract art. Don't try to create something realistic, but try to still make them recognizable as an athlete.

Design an advertisement for a café using the surrealist art style. Look at the work of Salvador Dalí or René Magritte for inspiration.

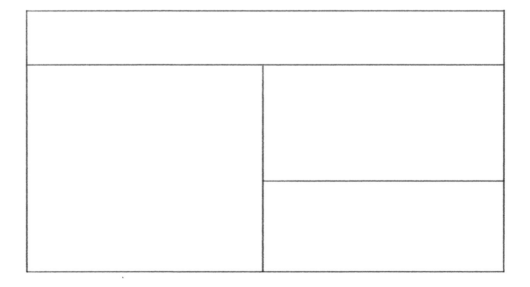

Create a landscape or scene that takes place in the summer. You can be literal and show an outdoor setting, or more figurative and portray a scene that evokes the feelings of this season.

Create a piece of abstract art on the theme of outer space. You could depict planets, space vehicles and technology, astronauts, stars, other celestial bodies, or anything that comes to mind.

Give new meaning to the word "cubicle" by turning this office space into a cubist illustration. You can look at the works of Juan Gris, Georges Braque, and Pablo Picasso for inspiration.

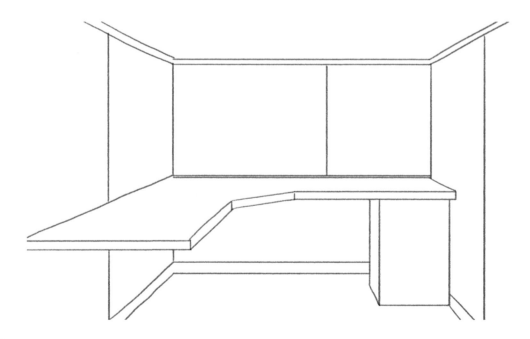

Draw your own face here, but be abstract and weird with it. You could try matching the style of the example or do something very different.

What was the highlight of your day yesterday? Imagine that something or someone tried to stop you from experiencing it. Write a paragraph about what they did and how you reacted.

Illustrate this type with art that makes it appear as if the letters themselves are made of wood that has been washed up on the shore.

Add a jogger to this scene, limiting yourself to only ten lines. Prioritize thoughtfully so you can convey motion and meaning.

Create a piece of abstract art depicting a boxing match, using basic shapes and lines. How can you add a sense of weight to the movements?

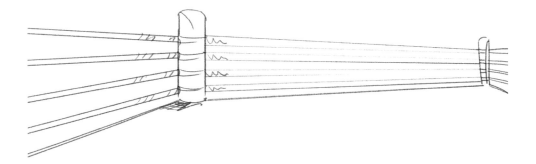

Parakeets can have a variety of colors and patterns on their feathers that can be depicted many ways depending on what you want to show. Fill in this bird with a proper coat of feathers, using whatever techniques and media you're in the mood for.

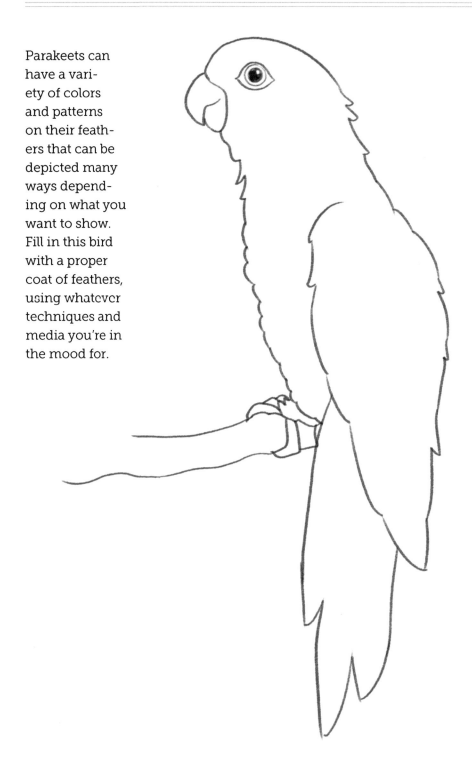

Using any shading technique you wish, add dimension and light to these simple shapes to create the effect of a single, consistent light source.

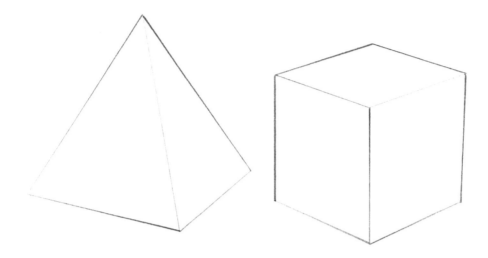

Add something drifting in space. Is it a rocket? A UFO? An astronaut, alien, or something else entirely? You could even choose to focus on creating an otherworldly galaxy using texture or patterns.

Using color, lines, and/or any techniques you wish, fill in and perhaps surround or enhance this word art to show your own interpretation of how the word makes you feel.

DELICIOUS

Stippling involves using many dots of the same color and size, placed in different densities, to create a shading effect. It works especially well for close-ups of easily recognized objects. Use stippling to fill in this potted plant.

Give this house windows, perhaps using a ruler to help guide your lines and keep them straight. If you have time, you could add textures to the roof or sides to further hone your depiction of perspective.

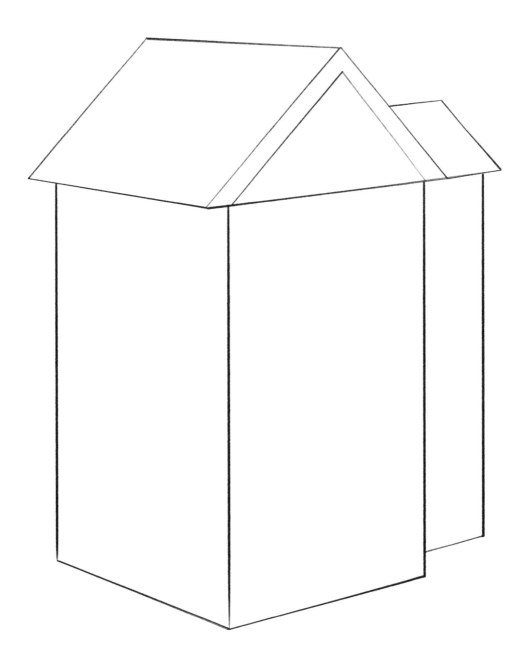

A kitchen is often a place of comfort. Draw an illustration of your kitchen here, or design your ideal cooking space.

Add to this city scene in a surrealist style. Surrealist art includes unpredictable, illogical elements that all contribute to dreamlike imagery that feels strange and unfamiliar.

Add a shell for this snail, but make it something unusual, unexpected, or even fantastical.

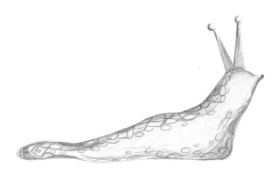

Finish illustrating
a dandelion. You
could try depict-
ing it in full
bloom with all its
petals, or after
the seeds have
become puff-
balls, or perhaps
even show them
floating away.

If you're working with color, try filling in each of these rectangles with the color and/or gradient that the lines inside it evoke for you. Or add to them in a way that accents what is already here.

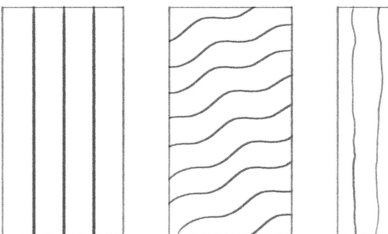
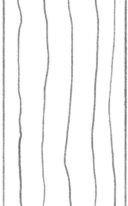

Using color, lines, and any other techniques you wish, fill in or surround this word art with imagery to reflect the word and how it makes you feel.

Design a spacecraft that uses a large rocket to blast off. You could take inspiration from real-life space travel, your favorite sci-fi story, or something else.

Create a piece of abstract art on the theme of a party to remember. Rely more on shapes, lines, and color rather than detail or shading. Think about how to frame your illustration in a unique way that captures your impressions of the experience.

Think back on some wild or unusual hairstyles you've seen, had, or considered, and put them on these mannequins.

Using whatever techniques you wish, make this type actually look three-dimensional.

Crosshatching means drawing lines that intersect, using different thicknesses and spacing between them to create shading. Practice your crosshatching here.

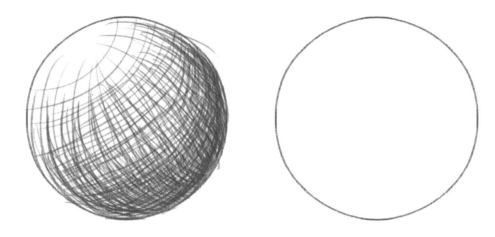

Pick a song you love and look up its sheet music. Transfer the staff lines and notes onto this page—not as a direct copy, but using color and size to express how the song makes you feel.

Create a piece of abstract art on the theme of a night in the big city. Rely more on shapes, lines, and color rather than detail or shading. Think about how to frame your illustration in a unique way that captures your impressions of the city at night.

Depict a bird's wing here with some detail. You could use fine lines to create many individual feathers, go more expressionist, or even just focus on colors.

Add the title you'd like to receive. Try to make your word art appear to follow the curve of the mug, and give it a dynamic sense of style and/or color.

Create a piece of abstract art on the theme of a trip to the beach. Rely more on shapes, lines, and color rather than detail or shading. Think about how to frame your illustration in a unique way that captures your impressions of the experience.

Fill out this pine
forest so that the
trees appear to
be farther and
farther away.

Illustrate this type with art that reflects
how you feel when you're on cloud nine.

Depict a statue of a person, character, or creature using just one color. You could draw an existing statue or figurine you've seen or have, or create something new. How can you make the subject recognizable using its shape and shading alone rather than relying on details and color?

Bubble tea is made with milk tea and lots of dark, chewy tapioca balls. Draw a cup and fill it with a flavor you love or one you'd like to try—and don't forget the tapioca balls.

Bat wings are distinctly different from bird wings. Try adding the wings to this furry flying friend, the fruit bat.

Using color, lines, and/or any techniques you wish, fill in and perhaps surround or enhance this word art to show how the word makes you feel.

Imagine what it's like to view Earth from orbit (feel free to look up a reference) and show our planet from this view, taking into account the sun's rays.

Illustrate this type in a way that makes it appear as if the word itself is mutating and changing form.

MUTATION

Create a landscape or scene that takes place in the spring. You can be literal and show an outdoor setting, or more figurative and portray a scene that evokes the feelings of this season.

Illustrate a lighthouse standing watch on this cliff face. You could focus on detailed shading or use color to portray a particular time of day or weather.

When you think about the ideal breakfast, what comes to mind? Show it here. Don't forget something to drink, and the utensils you'll need.

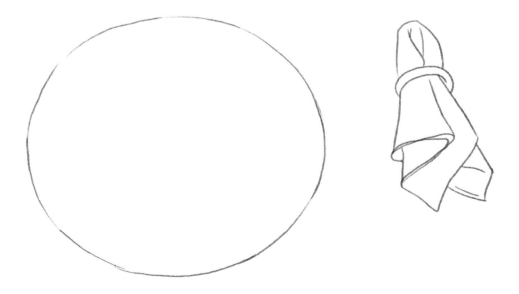

Grass can be used to give depth and dimension to so many types of images. Fill this page with grass illustrated in different ways—try various species, styles, colors, and/or media.

Design an eye-catching menu with only a handful of options. Give it a unique theme and think of what menu items would satisfy despite the few choices.

Complete this image to go along with the phrase "slam dunk."

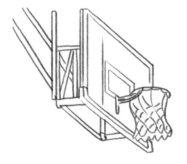

If you live near a coast, gather some interesting seashells for reference; otherwise, look up photographs online or in a book. Draw or paint your favorite seashells, paying attention to the shape and texture of each one.

Using color, lines, and/or any techniques you wish, fill in and perhaps surround or enhance this word art to show what feelings the word inspires.

Complete this
image to show
what you think is
number one.

Fill in the details of this moon. You could use color, shading, lines, or do something abstract or surreal.

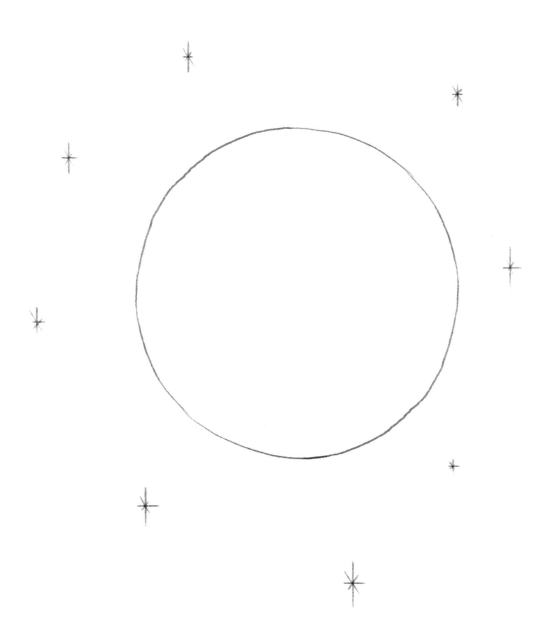

Fill in this plaque with the portrait of someone you imagine would receive this award.

Complete this image to show a close finish. It could be horses racing, people, dogs, or something weird like ice cream cones.

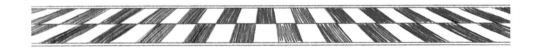

Illustrate this type with art to make it appear as if the words themselves are in different phases of being forged.

Add texture and lighting to the asteroids in this field. You can decide where the source of light is coming from. Perhaps try practicing your shading or crosshatching.

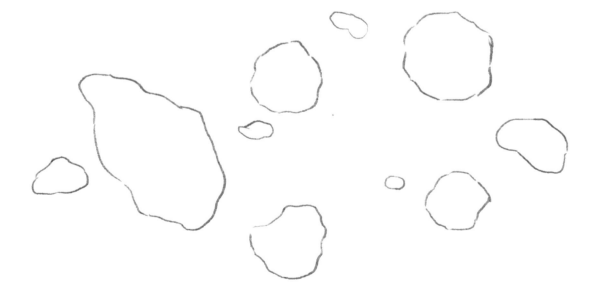

Design a flag for a group you're in, or used to be in, or one you would like to create. What kinds of symbols, patterns, and/or colors would represent it well?

Complete this image to illustrate the phrase "a strange development."

Depict a close-up of a daffodil in full bloom to complete the bunch. You can focus on shading and details or emphasize mood using color.

Using color, lines, and/or any techniques you wish, fill in and perhaps surround or enhance this word art to show what feelings the word inspires.

Take a small, oddly shaped object, such as a tangled charging cable, and place it on your page—ideally in a place where light will cast a shadow on the sheet. Now, with your imagination and some creativity, use the object's shape, and/or its shadow, to create an image of something else.

Fill in the spaces on this control panel to include extra buttons, knobs, dials, and/or switches. Include at least one convex and one concave button, with labels to show what they do.

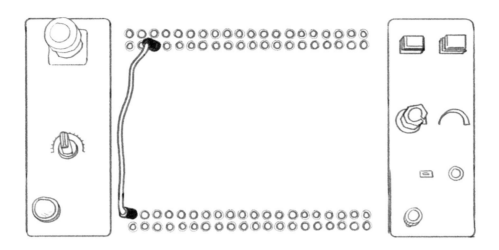

Using color, lines, and/or any techniques you wish, fill in and perhaps surround or enhance this word art to show what feelings the word inspires.

A beehive's honeycombs are created using a repeating pattern—called tessellation. Try creating an interlocking pattern for a new honeycomb here.

Linocut art entails carving lines and shapes into pieces of linoleum to create a printable image with a distinctive blocky style. Replicating the linocut style, add texture and patterns to this background to make it look like a backdrop for a theater set.

Design a tablecloth pattern. Try to keep it simple enough to repeat consistently without difficulty, but otherwise, use any colors, techniques, or patterns you wish.

Add another fern to go along with the example. You could also use color or add style to the example, depending on what you create.

Create an advertisement for an imaginary destination featuring your own invented language. Think of how basic shapes are used to form letters as you design your own.

Add a freshly chopped ingredient to this scene, portraying it split into sections. A fruit or vegetable would be perfect.

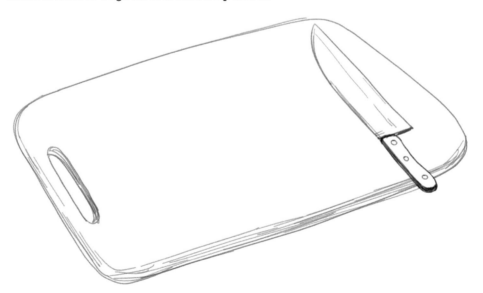

Illustrate a naturalistic lizard resting in this space. It can be any species you wish, and if you are having trouble deciding, feel free to be vague and more expressive. Consider how to portray the texture of its skin.

Illustrate a piece of fruit in color but use a totally different shade than its real color. How does capturing realistic shading with a different color change your perception of the object?

What goals and dreams did you have when you were younger? Did you pursue those dreams? How might you have changed them or let them go?

Design a new denomination for a currency note. Who or what is on the front? How much is it worth?

Create a landscape or scene that takes place in winter. You can be literal and show an outdoor setting, or more figurative and portray a scene that evokes the feelings of this season.

Illustrate a scene here of a painting accident, using colors if you'd like. If you're using a single pen or pencil, try to create an ink spill. Either way, think of how paint or ink might splash and land across the floor.

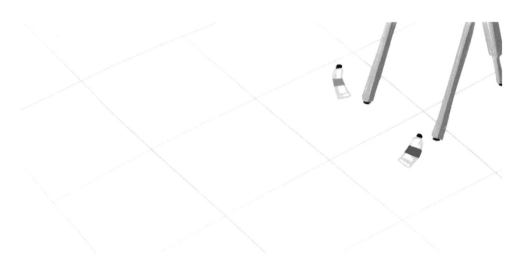

Add some kelp or other underwater vegetation to this scene. You can use colors and blending to create a vibrant mood, or focus more on the detailed shapes of plants swaying in the water.

Add a design to this pennant. It can have whatever theme you'd like. You could design a logo, re-create something you've seen, or even try to make it look hand-stitched.

Using color, lines, and/or any techniques you wish, fill in and perhaps surround or enhance this word art to show how this word makes you feel.

Illustrate a scene from an insect's point of view, close to the ground. Consider things like grass, flowers, pebbles, dirt, or even other insects—all of which would look different from this perspective.

Add a boat floating on these gentle waters. It could be a simple rowboat or a larger vessel seen from far away.

Add a snow-
boarder to this
scene, in the
middle of
making a trail.
Try to put them
in a pose that fits
with the motion
implied by
that trail.

A person has been commanded to accomplish a noble task. Depict them kneeling before a throne. Are they a knight, a queen, a warrior, or someone else altogether? You decide who to portray.

Fill in the rays of light from this sun. You could use colors to create the effect, or lines, or both. Try to make something stylized rather than realistic.

Add foliage to this tree, but instead of trying to draw every single leaf, try depicting large swatches of leaves in a stylized way. Use different shades for different patches, and layer them one over another.

Portray the scene and weather at this bus stop on a dreary day.

Using pointillism, add shading and texture to this old tin cup.

Using color, lines, and/or any techniques you wish, fill in and perhaps surround or enhance this word art to show what feelings the word inspires.

ACHIEVEMENT

Using only straight lines, create an image of one or more objects that are known for being round and curvy. How can you depict them in a stylized way that makes what they are apparent?

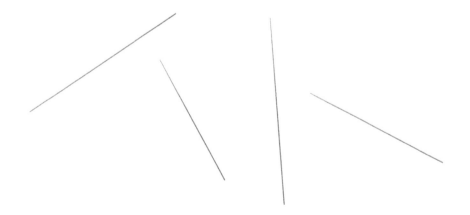

Create a landscape or scene that takes place in autumn. You can be literal and show an outdoor setting, or more figurative and portray a scene that evokes the feelings of this season.

Use the crosshatching technique (creating depth and shading with parallel lines) to add shading to these glass bottles.

Use crosshatching to add shading to this pie and the windowsill it's resting on.

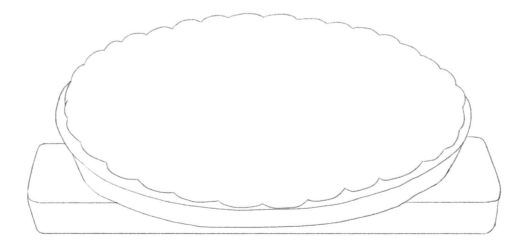

Fill in this mandala, trying to make it symmetrical in every direction. You could use colors, shading, and gradients to give it life. Or, with a single color, flesh out the design into something more intricate.

Hills are a common background element, so it can be useful to work on your technique for drawing them. Using color and/or detail, add life to these rolling hills.

Add chess pieces to this board. You could focus on simple designs with more detail and shading, try filling out depth with multiple pieces in the background and foreground, or have fun designing some themed pieces.

Using color, lines, and/or any techniques you wish, fill in and perhaps surround or enhance this word art to show what feelings the word inspires.

FREEZING

Give this surfer a big wave to ride using whatever techniques and/or color style you prefer.

Finish this metalwork sculpture. Will you create something abstract or representational?

This little bird needs a cozy nest to sleep in. Add one in the tree.

Grow some mushrooms around this old tree stump. If you're using color, make it a night scene with mushrooms that are glowing.

Add a wandering merchant on a long journey. What kind of clothing are they wearing? What objects or equipment are they holding?

Illustrate this type with art that makes it look as if it's melting into a puddle.

MELTING

In this scene, add a singer holding the microphone and singing into it. Consider what kind of performer they are and what song they might be singing.

In Asian folklore, the rabbit is associated with the moon because the light and dark parts of the moon can resemble an image of a rabbit. Create your own interpretation of this moon-rabbit imagery.

Using these triangles as a base, create some abstract art. Perhaps use just triangles as a recurring element, or add other shapes.

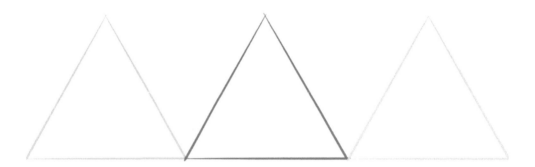

Give this cat a tail and ears, but make them strange, wild, and bizarre.

Fill in this solar system by designing some planets. Use color and/or shading to make it look like something you'd find in a textbook, but feel free to be creative. Perhaps you could add a large meteorite, satellite, or something else.

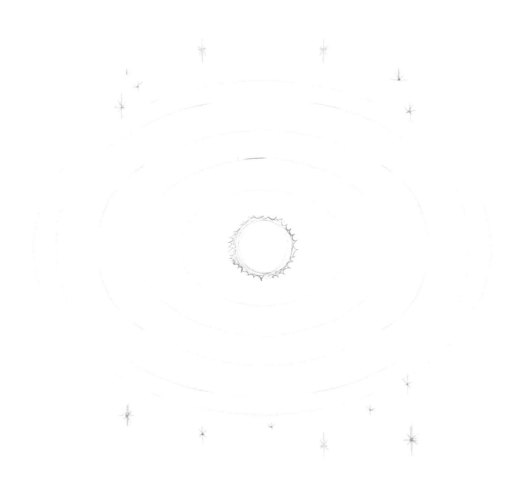

Imagine a secluded cabin on a lake. Make the scene as expressive as possible, taking inspiration from impressionist artists such as Mary Cassatt.

Give this Chihuahua a body that's not what one would expect.

Give musical life to these instruments by surrounding them with music notes, waves of sound, and any effects that will make them appear to be creating music. What kind of song do you want to express around them?

Place yourself, in
this mirror,
holding an item
and reacting to
it in some way.
Try not to stress
about being
photorealistic
unless that's
specifically what
you choose to
go for.

Awaken this ancient relic by adding light, runes, and effects to make it appear to be activated by a mystical force.

Add detail to this car. You can concentrate on texture and finish with reflections or design a unique decal.

Give wings to this butterfly, but don't limit yourself to something known or realistic. Use this as an opportunity to get creative. Create a unique species of strange butterfly, or do something special with its colors and patterns.

Using color, lines, and/or any techniques you wish, fill in and perhaps surround or enhance this word art to show what feelings the word inspires.

BOILING

Give these clouds shading and texture. Try to use blending to give the illustration a softer tone and consider how to portray a consistent light source.

Choose any of the planets or moons in our solar system and illustrate it here. You could emphasize what we can see on its surface, do something more impressionistic, or put more energy into mood, color, and background.

Give this sidewalk texture and detail. You could even add a crack or two if you wish. Try to fill in some space to create a darker shade, using the negative space to portray texture.

Transform this into a huge dragon kite and make it look as if it's flying in a strong wind.

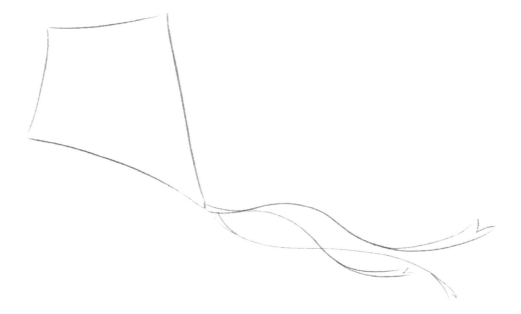

Find a photo of a delicious meal you've had recently (or search online for a photo of that dish) and re-create it with abstract shapes and patterns.

Study the wooden texture of a desk or table and try to create that kind of texture here. Add some graffiti carving for extra flavor.

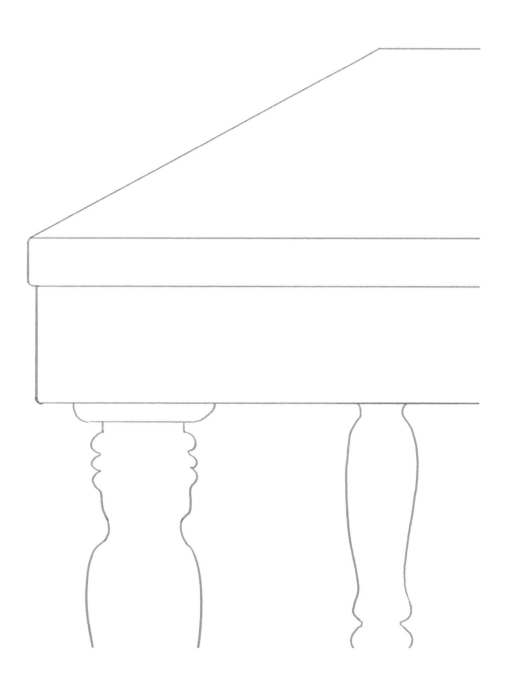

Add the toppings for these pizza slices. You could choose realistic ingredients or draw something totally experimental or wacky.

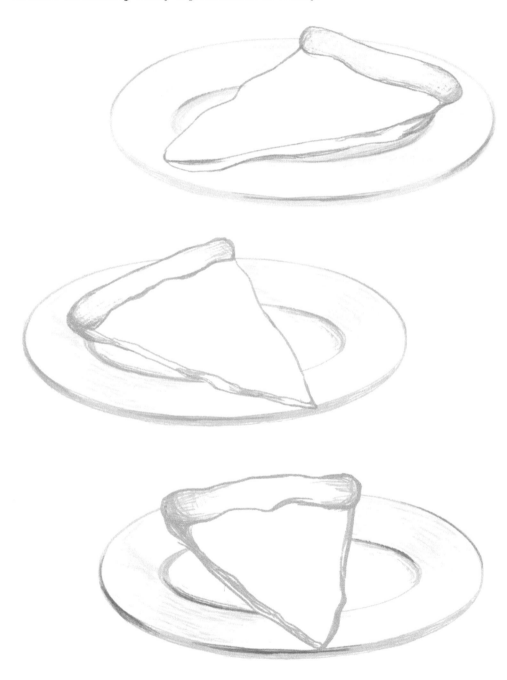

Add soda, beer, champagne, or something else fizzy or foamy to these glasses. How can you add detail to depict what kind of liquid is inside?

Show what is radiating this shine. Use whatever techniques you wish to give it a strong effect.

Practice your still life skills by drawing a muffin. Feel free to use a reference. Think of how you can use color, shading, or any other techniques to give dimensionality to the muffin, and how textured it can be.

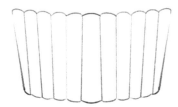

When you think of balloons, what comes to mind? Write about a vivid memory you have that involves one or more of them.

Give this log cabin shading and detail to portray a time of day.
You could also give the logs a rich texture.

Try your hand at some light architectural work by designing a workplace area you might like to use. You might use a ruler to keep straight lines and consistent distances, but it's fine if you play it loose. Don't forget a restroom.

Add people to this city scene, creating a sense of what time of day it is. How busy is it? Rather than dwelling on identifying details for the people, focus instead on their overall shape and pose, body language, and what they might be doing.

Give this scene some high-contrast shading, illuminated by the fire, so this weary traveler can get some rest after a long day.

Figuring out a way to depict water can be tricky but rewarding. Practice drawing a still pond of water with a single stone falling in, creating ripples. Try depicting the moment the stone hits the water, or focus more on the ripples spreading out. Use a bit of shading to show the way light reflects off the ripples.

Design a cassette tape label. You can re-create the style of a particular era or genre of music, or give it a handmade mixtape vibe. Include the title of the album and the band name.

Depict an ideal fishing spot for this person to find a nice catch—
a pond, a lake, or even someplace otherworldly.

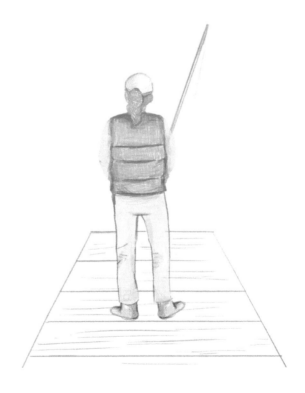

Give shading and sheen to this metal blade so it looks nice and sharp.

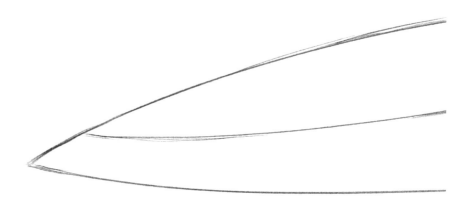

Fill out the picnic scene here, but make it one that has been invaded by some type of wildlife.

Use this space to illustrate the theme "dog walk."

Create a piece of abstract art on the theme of a day at the bakery. Rely more on shapes, lines, and color rather than detail or shading. Think about how to frame your illustration in a unique way that captures your impressions of a bakery.

This figure is reaching the light at the end of a dark tunnel. Use shading to highlight how bright the light is and to cast a long shadow behind them.

Add a pair of matching ice sculptures to this scene. Capture a chilled, reflective tone that is regal enough for a fancy ball.

Illustrate a cover for a retro comic book.

Decorate these donuts. Frosting, glaze, sprinkles, filling oozing out . . .
you could even give them a common theme.

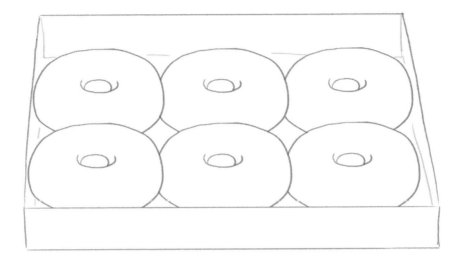

Add a digitized tree, person, or creature to this alternate plane of reality.

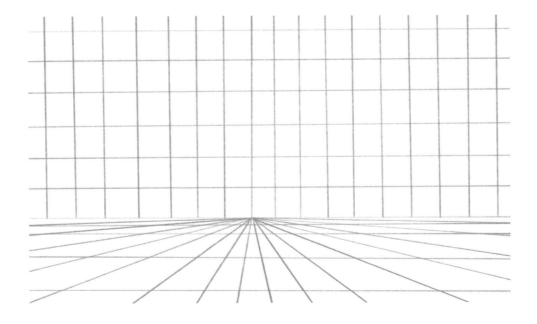

Fill in this scrapbook by depicting some special moments from a particular day, time, or place in your life that gives you positive feelings. The items don't all have to be photos and can include mementos or souvenirs like a movie ticket, a newspaper clipping, or anything else.

Add the design of your favorite sports team to this jersey—or, if you're not into sports, make a team up and give them a design and logo. Consider including color to make it stand out.

Draw your name on this sticker in a stylized way. Make it flashy or noticeable, but use just one color.

Even if you don't care for golf, the courses can be beautiful. Curate some beauty for this golf course.

Draw snow across the branches of this tree. Try to add shading or shimmering to the snow to make it stand out.

Add shading and detail to this treasure chest. Which parts are metallic? You could try adding texture to make it appear wooden and weathered or rusted and old.

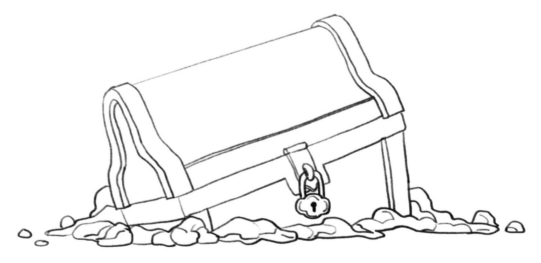

Illustrate a cactus using any medium that strikes your fancy. Think about how to make it particularly prickly, with short, sharp spines.

Add texture to this tree's bark. It can be any type of tree you like. Think of what kind of medium or technique you can use to cover the space efficiently while capturing the organic texture.

Give this scene some fierce lightning and rain. You can go for more detailed, forked lightning or something more abstract and expressive. How will you depict rainfall? It doesn't have to be literal drops or straight lines.

Create a steampunk device at this bench. It could be a tool, a piece of equipment, or something to wear.

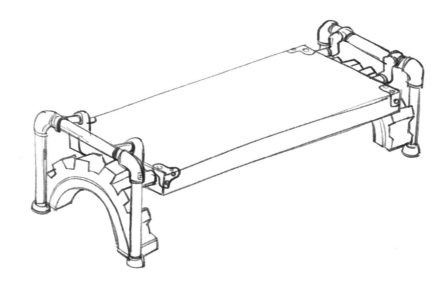

Pick a piece of furniture nearby, maybe even the chair you're sitting on. Break it down in your mind into the components it's made of. Rearrange them on the page to create a completely new piece of furniture.

Using the idea of "gooey," portray what this hand is holding. Try to feature some goo dripping down.

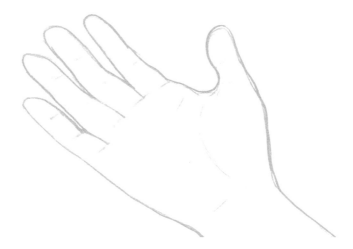

Give this train window a breathtaking view of a landscape. It could be a town, the sea, a mountain peak, forests, a snowy field, or even a beach.

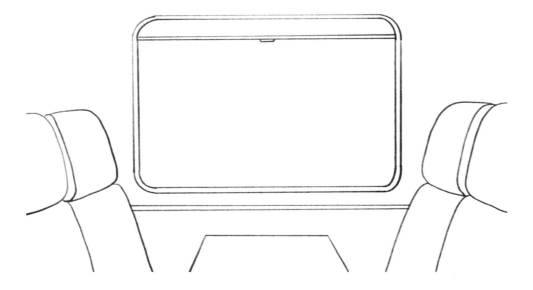

Create some street art advertising for a local restaurant. It could be a real restaurant you visit or just one you make up. Come up with some specials on offer and create a chalkboard feel for the menu, if you can.

Add the reflection on this person's sunglasses. What kind of scene are they viewing, and how can you make it look like a reflection across both lenses?

Try creating an imaginary friend this child is seeing. They could be realistic, fantastical, or even scary.

Add detail to this ice floe, and remember that lighting can be harsh in icy climates. You can also try depicting the parts of the ice that are below the water and how the water blurs them.

Add a critter peeking out of this tree trunk—maybe something that would take you by surprise.

Something has caused this traffic jam . . . and it's big. Add whatever is holding everyone up.

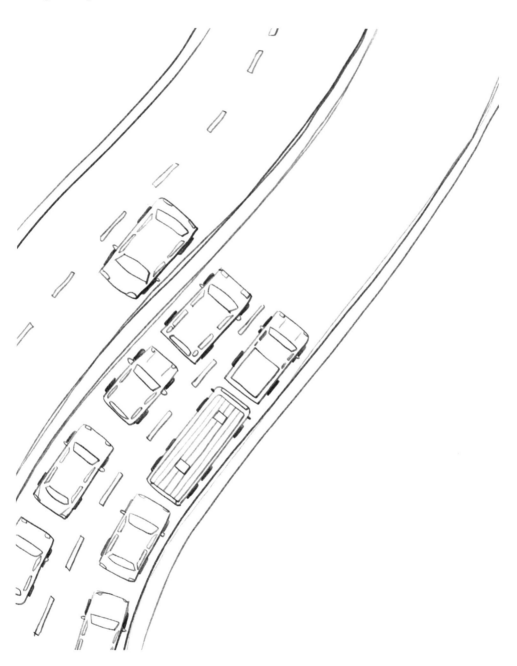

Add the silhouette of someone walking home late at night.

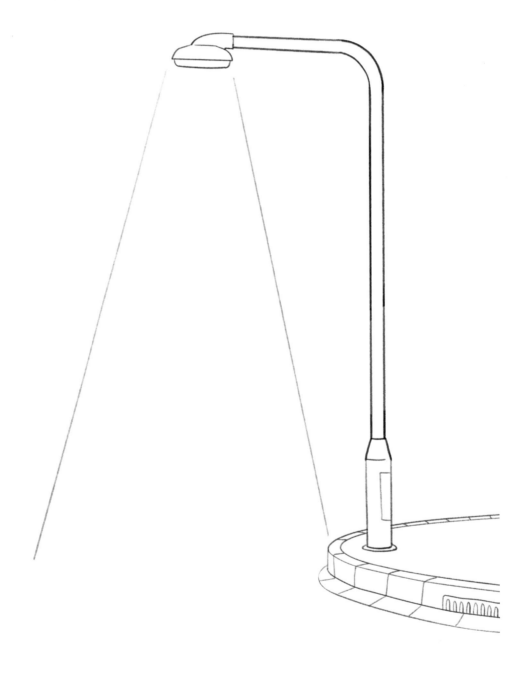

Spruce up this path by making it look like a candy-themed road. Think lollipops, candy canes, and gumdrops. Try using color, patterns, or shading to add some sparkle.

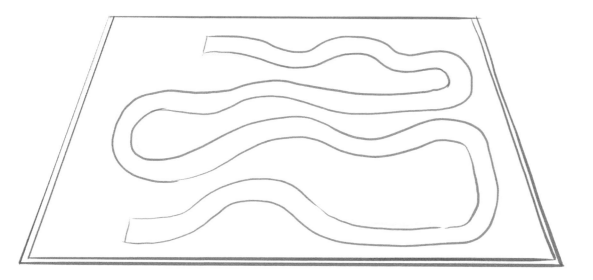

Turn these sticks into melting Popsicles. What kind of texture and flavor do they have?

Add the horizon to this beach scene. If you're using color, go for an ocean at sunset or at night, playing with color and shading. If you are sticking with a single color, perhaps this beach could be on a bay with another shore in the distance, and you could portray a coastal town and some details for the waves.

Add detail and shading to these chickens feeding. Create a sense of morning lighting as you include their feathers.

Add an assortment of freshly baked breads to this basket. Try to include a few different types. How can you make them look warm and fresh, or add texture to their rough crusts or soft insides?

We spend a lot of time where we sleep. Depict the space you sleep in here. If you feel it won't be interesting, perhaps look up a reference of a place to sleep or a nap that you'll have more fun illustrating.

Using the crosshatching technique, add some detailed shading to this old rotary phone.

Describe the home you grew up in using words related to each of the five senses—touch, taste, sight, sound, and smell.

Using color, lines, and/or any techniques you wish, fill in and perhaps surround or enhance this word art to show what feelings the word inspires.

STARLIGHT

Give this horse a rider. Think of how you can use the appearance of the person riding to convey a setting. You could always add something to the background to further illustrate that setting.

Add some bubbles floating through the air. You could try to create depth of field, a sense of movement (as if they're being blown around), or just try for light reflecting from a consistent source.

Add texture, color, and personality to this brick wall. You could always add something over the top of the wall, or simply focus on creating a consistent, detailed look.

Complete this monkey illustration, trying to mimic the style in which the face is drawn.

Practice your spatial skills by depicting this cylinder at different angles and rotations. Feel free to add a pattern to it for a challenge.

Draw the other half of this person's face, but depict an alternate identity or another side to them.

Illustrate an underwater creature. Invent something new or fantastical, perhaps by combining the traits of several existing species.

Using the lines that are already here, connect them, work around them, fill in shapes, or do something else to create some kind of household object or scene.

Using color, lines, and/or any techniques you wish, fill in and perhaps surround or enhance this word art to show what feelings the word inspires.

INDUSTRY

Add some commonly used tools from your toolbox to this worktable, or a set of tools you wouldn't expect to see used together.

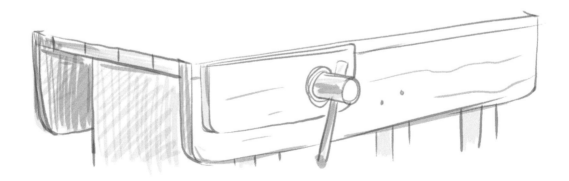

Think of how smoke is different from clouds and illustrate some smoke billowing from this chimney.

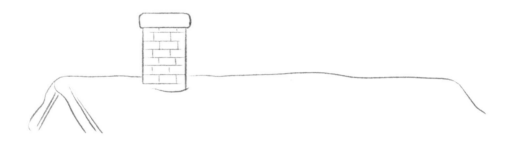

Make this throw blanket look relaxing and cozy. You could focus on a pattern or design, or concentrate on creating a rich texture.

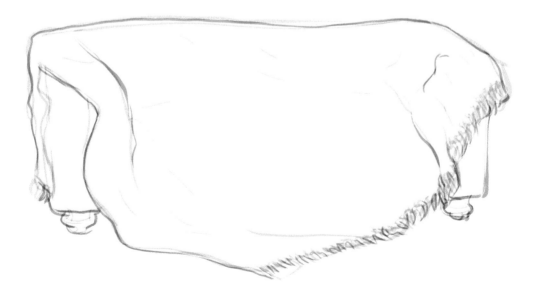

Take a book with a cover you find visually interesting and use this space to depict it as a still life object. Ideally, you'll want to illustrate it from an angle rather than head-on from the front.

Give details to this eye. What kinds of shading or coloring could you use to give it personality?

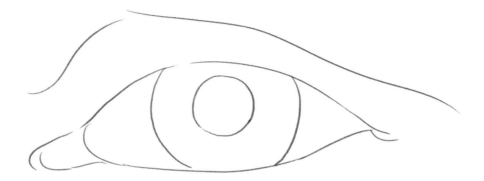

Add texture to each of these three cubes so they feel distinct. For example, you could make one grassy or furry, another metallic, and another wooden.

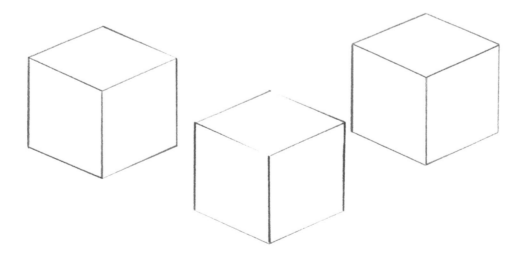

Using color, lines, and/or any techniques you wish, fill in and perhaps surround or enhance this word art to show what feelings the word inspires.

Add a reflection to this rainy puddle. Something as simple as a cloudy sky is fine, but feel free to experiment. Consider the raindrops falling and how they might shift the surrounding reflection.

Use two distinct colors for this prompt (if you only have one, use two very different shades). Try designing a poster that conveys a motivational message. If you're struggling to come up with an idea, you could re-create one that already exists.

Design the labels for three cans containing something—maybe something you wouldn't usually find in a can.

Add to this setting in a style inspired by Japanese woodblock paintings to create a peaceful scene. (Feel free to look up some references for style.)

Create an expressionist illustration of a portrait of yourself or someone else. You can look to Edvard Munch and Henri Matisse for inspiration.

Stumping is a practice that uses blending to create shading. You can use your finger, a cotton swab, a rag, or something similar. Practice your stumping here to finish the image.

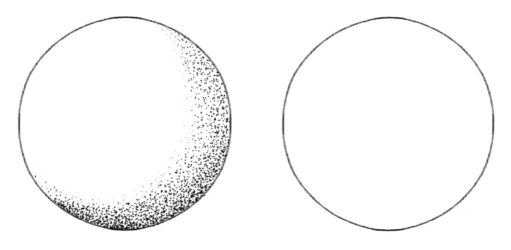

Imagine a city or building made of crystals and ice. Depict it below, relying on straight edges and pointed ends.

Show what this hand is reluctant to touch.

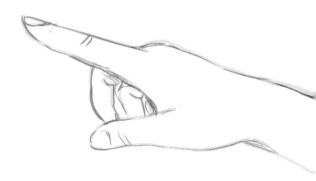

Using the lines here, draw one long, single line that connects them all together to form the image of an item in your own home.

Using any type of shading technique, create the atmosphere of a sunset.

Take this illustration of a camera and try to remake it in a 1960s pop art style. Think of Andy Warhol and Roy Lichtenstein's art for inspiration.

Illustrate the details created by this disco ball. Think of how color and lighting can be used with the many small, reflective pieces.

Create the logo of a fancy 1920s-era bar, shop, or restaurant. Include both text and a symbol or image.

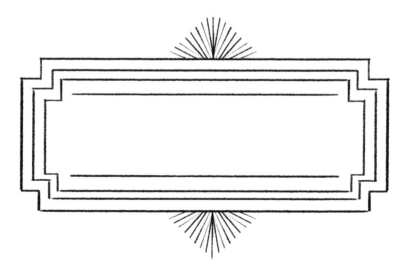

Illustrate an article of clothing made of something soft and unexpected—for example, a helmet made of cotton balls.

Using a pointillist style, add shading to these shapes to make them look three-dimensional.

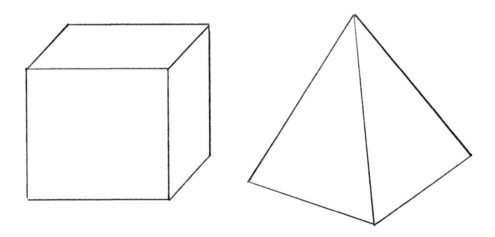

Depict a candle burning, thinking of how a flickering flame can be captured in a moment, as well as how to portray the dim light of a candle in the dark. Is it close to a wall? Being held by a hand? How is the light playing on what is around it, including the candlestick?

Design your own food truck. What kind of patterns or colors does it have? What food is it selling?

Pick your favorite breed of dog and illustrate the face in a geometric style, using straight lines and sharp angles to re-create the breed in a recognizable way.

Stack some snacks onto this cone that you wouldn't expect to find in an ice cream parlor.

You've just returned from the mage's market. Stock your witch's or wizard's cupboard with magic potions and mystical ingredients.

Draw a stack of history books. Make each one look different, including the way their titles are written. Create a set of themed books around a single topic, imagine historical fantasy subjects, or re-create real books.

What was one major epiphany of self-discovery you've had about yourself? How did coming to this realization help you reshape yourself, your life, your beliefs, or your behaviors?

Think back on a pivotal moment in your life, something that changed you and defined who you've become. Now try illustrating that moment here. It doesn't have to be a literal re-creation. Consider what kinds of imagery you can use in a collage that evokes the importance of that moment, or perhaps use another stylized way to depict it.

Complete this word art using whatever media, techniques, tools, and themes you wish, as long as it expresses how you show love to yourself.